Purpose: The purpose of this story is to provide basic reading for children ages 2 and up. Please feel free to contact me at littleyapper.com for comments.

About the author: Jane Thai is a Chinese American author, designer and educator. These days, you will find her drawing and writing children's books. She draws her inspiration from her students and her daughter. Jane lives in the Big Apple with her husband, daughter and 4 yorkies.

To learn more go to : Littleyapper.com

Dedication: to Julia & Tate

I belong to:

I like pickles.

我 喜欢 酸 黄瓜.
wǒ xǐhuān suān huángguā

吃

What do you like to eat?

你 喜欢 吃 什么?
nǐ xǐhuān chī shénme

" I like to eat flies," says the frog.

青蛙 说:"我 喜欢 吃 苍蝇."
qīngwā shuō wǒ xǐhuān chī cāngyíng

" I like to eat poop," says the fly.

苍蝇 说: "我 喜欢 吃 粪便."
cāngyíng shuō   wǒ xǐhuān chī fènbiàn

"I like to eat bananas," says the monkey.

猴子 说:"我 喜欢 吃 香蕉."
hóuzi shuō　wǒ xǐhuān chī xiāngjiāo

" I like to eat pickle sandwiches," says Bobby.

波比 说:"我 喜欢 吃 酸 黄瓜 三明治."
bō bǐ shuō　wǒ xǐhuān chī suān huángguā sānmíngzhì

喝

What do you like to drink?

你 喜欢 喝 什么?
nǐ xǐhuān hē shénme

"I like to drink water," says the hippopotamus.

河马 说："我 喜欢 喝 水."
hémǎ shuō   wǒ xǐhuān hē shuǐ

"I like to drink milk," says the cat.

猫 说:" 我 喜欢 喝 牛奶."
māo shuō　　wǒ xǐhuān hē niúnǎi

"I like to drink nectar," says the butterfly.

蝴蝶 说：" 我 喜欢 喝 花蜜."
húdié shuō　wǒ xǐhuān hē huāmì

" I like to drink pickle juice," says Bobby.

波比 说:" 我 喜欢 喝 酸 黄瓜 汁."
bō bǐ shuō wǒ xǐhuān hē suān huángguā zhī

玩

What do you like to play?

你 喜欢 玩 什么?
nǐ xǐhuān wán shénme?

" I like to play ball," says the dog.

狗 说：" 我 喜欢 打 球."
gǒu shuō　　wǒ xǐhuān dǎ　qiú

" I like to play with the fish," says the cat.

猫 说:"我 喜欢 跟 鱼 玩."
māo shuō　　wǒ xǐhuān gēn yú wán

BOO!

" I like to play peek-a-boo," says the baby.

宝宝 说:"我 喜欢 玩 躲 猫 猫."
bǎobao shuō　wǒ xǐhuān wán duǒ māo māo

"I like to play drums with pickles," says Bobby.

波比 说:" 我 喜欢 用 酸 黄瓜 打鼓."
bō bǐ shuō　wǒ xǐhuān yòng suān huángguā dǎ gǔ

What do you like to do?

你 喜欢 做 什么?
nǐ xǐhuān zuò shénme

" I like to sleep," says the pig.

猪 说：" 我 喜欢 睡觉."
zhū shuō wǒ xǐhuān shuìjiào

" I like to hop," says the rabbit.

兔子 说 :" 我 喜欢 跳跃."
tùzǐ shuō wǒ xǐhuān tiàoyuè

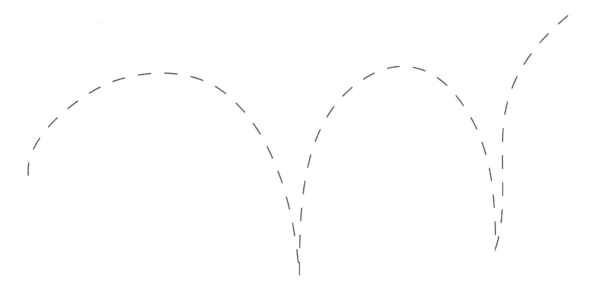

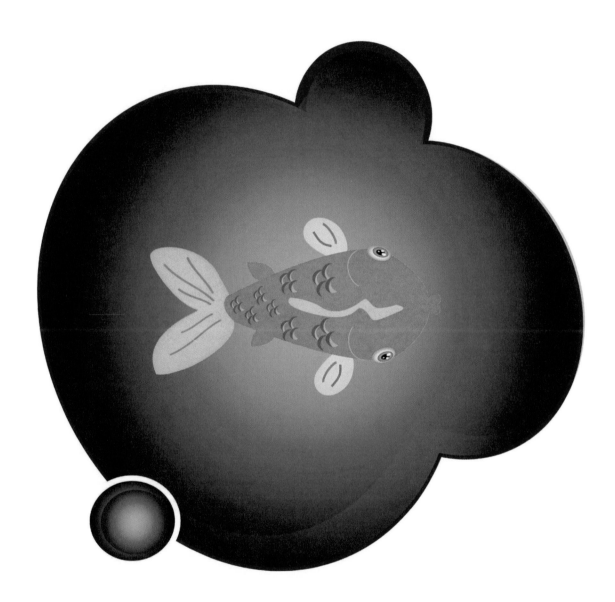

" I like to swim," says the goldfish.

金鱼 说:" 我 喜欢 游泳."
jīnyú shuō wǒ xǐhuān yóuyǒng

" I like to go bobbing for pickles," says Bobby.

波比 说:"我 喜欢 玩 从　水桶 里咬 酸　黄瓜
bō bǐ shuō　wǒ xǐhuān wán cóng shuǐtǒng lǐ yǎo suān huángguā

出来 的 游戏."
chūlái de　yóuxì

Bobby really likes pickles.

波比真的很喜欢 酸 黄瓜.
Bō bǐ zhēn de hěn xǐhuān suān huángguā.

THE
END

故事结束
gùshì jiéshù

Vocabulary Learning 词汇

I 我 wǒ

to like 喜欢 xǐhuān

pickles 酸黄瓜 suān huángguā

to eat 吃 chī

to drink 喝 hē

to play 玩 wán

to do 做 zuò

frog 青蛙 qīngwā

fly 苍蝇 cāngyíng

monkey 猴子 hóuzi

banana 香蕉 xiāngjiāo

hippopotamus 河马 hémǎ

water 水 shuǐ

dog 狗 gǒu

cat 猫 māo

milk 牛奶 niúnǎi

to hit 打 dǎ

ball 球 qiú

fish 鱼 yú

swim 游泳 yóuyǒng

baby 宝宝 bǎobǎo

drums 鼓 gǔ

pig 猪 zhū

sleep 睡觉 shuìjiào

rabbit 兔子 tùzǐ

to hop 跳跃 tiàoyuè

what 什么 shénme

peek-a-boo 躲猫猫 duǒ māo māo

you 你 nǐ

sandwich 三明治 sānmíngzhì

butterfly 蝴蝶 húdié

nectar 花蜜 huāmì

pickle juice 酸黄瓜汁 suān huángguā zhī

If you have enjoyed this story, please share and leave me a comment at littleyapper.com. A review on Amazon.com would be appreciated as well.
Thank you. 谢谢

Use code : **FIRSTWORDS** to download your FREE audio book and find out more tips on dual language learning at **littleyapper.com**

Other dual language books by Jane Thai

The Apple Tree
How Mommy Carries Her Baby
How the World got its Color from the Sea
12 Months of the Year
First Words in Chinese

48417539R00031

Made in the USA
Middletown, DE
14 June 2019